TSUBASA

CLAMP

TRANSLATED AND ADAPTED BY
William Flanagan

LETTERED BY
Dana Hayward

Published in the United Kingdom by Tanoshimi in 2006

1 3 5 7 9 10 8 6 4 2

First published in Japan by Kodansha Ltd., Tokyo in 2003. Copyright © 2003 by CLAMP.

Published by arrangement with Kodansha Ltd., Tokyo and with Del Rey, an imprint of Random House Inc., New York

Tanoshimi
The Random House Group Limited
20 Vauxhall Bridge Road, London, SW1V 2SA

Random House Australia (Pty) Limited
20 Alfred Street, Milsons Point, Sydney
New South Wales 2061, Australia

Random House New Zealand Limited
18 Poland Road, Glenfield
Auckland 10, New Zealand

Random House (Pty) Limited
Isle of Houghton, Corner of Boundary Road & Carse O'Gowrie
Houghton 2198, South Africa

Random House Publishers India Private Limited
301 World Trade Tower, Hotel Intercontinental Grand Complex,
Barakhamba Lane, New Delhi 110 001, India

Random House Group Limited Reg. No. 954009

www.tanoshimi.tv
www.randomhouse.co.uk

A CIP catalogue record for this book is available from the British Library

Papers used by Random House
are natural, recyclable products made from wood grown in sustainable forests.
The manufacturing processes conform to the environmental regulations of the country of origin.

ISBN 9780099504146 (from Jan 2007)
ISBN 0 09 950414 6

Printed and bound in Germany by GGP Media GmbH, Pößneck

Translator and Adaptor — William Flanagan
Lettering — Dana Hayward

Contents

Honorifics

Throughout the Tanoshimi Manga books, you will find Japanese honorifics left intact in the translations. For those not familiar with how the Japanese use honorifics, and more important, how they differ from English honorifics, we present this brief overview.

Politeness has always been a critical facet of Japanese culture. Ever since the feudal era, when Japan was a highly stratified society, use of honorifics — which can be defined as polite speech that indicates relationship or status — has played an essential role in the Japanese language. When addressing someone in Japanese, an honorific usually takes the form of a suffix attached to one's name (example: "Asuna-san"), or as a title at the end of one's name or in place of the name itself (example: "Negi-sensei," or simply "Sensei!").

Honorifics can be expressions of respect or endearment. In the context of manga and anime, honorifics give insight into the nature of the relationship between characters. Many translations into English leave out these important honorifics, and therefore distort the "feel" of the original Japanese. Because Japanese honorifics contain nuances that English honorifics lack, it is our policy at Tanoshimi not to translate them. Here, instead, is a guide to some of the honorifics you may encounter in Tanoshimi Manga.

-san: This is the most common honorific, and is equivalent to Mr., Miss, Ms., Mrs., etc. It is the all-purpose honorific and can be used in any situation where politeness is required.

-sama: This is one level higher than "-san." It is used to confer great respect.

-dono: This comes from the word "tono," which means "lord." It is an even higher level than "-sama," and confers utmost respect.

-kun: This suffix is used at the end of boys' names to express familiarity or endearment. It is also sometimes used by men among friends, or when addressing someone younger or of a lower station.

-chan: This is used to express endearment, mostly toward girls. It is also used for little boys, pets, and even among lovers. It gives a sense of childish cuteness.

Bozu: This is an informal way to refer to a boy, similar to the English term "kid".

Sempai: This title suggests that the addressee is one's "senior" in a group or organization. It is most often used in a school setting, where underclassmen refer to their upperclassmen as "sempai." It can also be used in the workplace, such as when a newer employee addresses an employee who has seniority in the company.

Kohai: This is the opposite of "sempai," and is used toward underclassmen in school or newcomers in the workplace. It connotes that the addressee is of lower station.

Sensei: Literally meaning "one who has come before," this title is used for teachers, doctors, or masters of any profession or art.

-[blank]:   Usually forgotten in these lists, but perhaps the most significant difference between Japanese and English. The lack of honorific means that the speaker has permission to address the person in a very intimate way. Usually, only family, spouses, or very close friends have this kind of permission. Known as *yobisute*, it can be gratifying when someone who has earned the intimacy starts to call one by one's name without an honorific. But when that intimacy hasn't been earned, it can also be very insulting.

RESERVoir CHRoNiCLE

Chapitre.14
Time to Get Under Way

4

YOU AREN'T WEAK!

STRENGTH AND WEAKNESS AREN'T MEASURED ONLY IN BATTLE.

GOING OUT AND DOING YOUR BEST FOR SOMEONE ELSE'S SAKE...

...IS A WONDERFUL SIGN OF STRENGTH.

GWI

THANKS!

THANK YOU!

SHÔGO-SAN!!

YO.

EH?!

HMP?

AHHH!

POK

HUHP

I'LL HAVE FUTA-MODAN.

AND A TORA-COLA.

OH! IT'S BEGINNING TO BURN. YOU'D BETTER EAT IT.

OF COURSE, SIR.

OKAY!

'SCUSE ME, WE'RE READY TO ORDER. I'LL HAVE TONPEI-YAKI!

I'M GLAD MY TEAM GETS GOOD INTELLIGENCE.

CAN YOU SKOOCH OVER A BIT?

HMP!

I TOLD YOU TO STOP THAT!!

YOUR MAJESTY?!

YOUR MAJESTY, REALLY?!

STAAARE

ONE FUTA-MODAN FOR THIS GENTLEMAN, YOUR MAJESTY!

YOUR MAJESTY!

6

IT'S OKAY.

IT WAS THE ONLY THING YOU COULD DO, CIRCUMSTANCES BEING WHAT THEY WERE.

I'M SORRY TO HAVE INTERRUPTED YOUR BATTLE.

NOBODY GOT WOUNDED, RIGHT?

WE'RE FINE.

I LOST 3000 TORA ON THAT!

I WON!

OH, SHUT UP!

BESIDES, I WAS LOSING THAT BATTLE BADLY.

MOKONA, I THINK YOUR TAIL IS A LITTLE BURNT.

KUROGANE IS TERRIBLE! HE MADE MOKONA GO "BOINK" FROM THE HEAT!

YOU STOLE MY FOOD AGAIN!

YOU LITTLE SLUG!

WE'LL HAVE TO GO TO A NEW WORLD... ERR... COUNTRY VERY SOON.

I SEE...

HOW LONG WILL YOU BE IN THE HANSHIN REPUBLIC?

SST

I'D HOPED TO MEET YOU IN OTHER PLACES THAN JUST BATTLE.

I WANTED TO GUIDE YOU AROUND TOWN A BIT.

PRIMELA WAS DISAPPOINTED, TOO.

GLNCH

8

I SURE WILL!!

BOUGHT THIS TOO.

THANK YOU SO MUCH!

GRN

BUT YOU HAVEN'T TASTED ALL OF THE COOKING THAT'S GENERATED THROUGH THE LOVE OF MY HONEY AND MYSELF!

YES.

YOU'RE GOING ALREADY?

RUBB

ARE YOU ALL RIGHT?

I'M STILL A LITTLE SLEEPY.

16

Chapitre.15
The Secret Country

I DON'T SEE ANYBODY STUPIDER THAN YOU.

GLANCE キョロ キョロ GLANCE

ゴッキーン

WHO ARE YOU CALLING STUPID?!

GRRRR

I AM THE ONLY SON OF THE RYANBAN-SAMA, THE MASTER OF THE COUNTRY OF KORYO *INCLUDING* THE TOWN OF RYONFI!

ぶるぶるぶる

GRWL GRWL GRWL GRWL

YOU INSULT ME?!

YOU LITTLE...

KRAA

DO YOU KNOW THE PUNISHMENT FOR OPPOSING THE RYANBAN?!

YOU DARE PUT DOWN MY FATHER?!

CHU'NYAN?!

GNCH

YOU MAY *CALL* HIM RYAN-BAN...

...BUT LESS THAN A YEAR AGO, HE WAS JUST A WANDERING SHINBAN MAGICIAN!

I CAN ONLY WISH THAT AMEN'OSA WOULD COME TO TOWN AS QUICKLY AS THEY CAN.

LOOK AT THESE GUYS!

RUNNING AMOK IN OUR MARKET!

THOSE ARE WEIRD CLOTHES!

STARE

HUSH
SH
SH

WHY DID YOU SUDDENLY...

MY HOUSE.

UM... WHERE ARE...

DON'T YOU HAVE SOMETHING TO SAY?

30

IT'S MITO-KÔMON!!

MITO...?

ひゃっほーい!
BOYOING

JUST THINK OF MOKONA AS A MASCOT.

OR MAYBE AN IDOL.

MOKONA IS MOKONA!!

BYOIINNG

WR

WOBBLE

AH!

YÛKO SAYS THAT THE FIRST GUY WHO PLAYED KÔMON-SAMA IS THE BEST!!

MOKONA'S AN IDOL!

TWRL

TWRL

MMMMM

RUBB RUBB RUBB

SO YOU THINK WE'RE THIS AMEN'OSA OF YOURS...

UM...

CHU'NYAN.

B-BMP B-BMP B-BMP

I'VE BEEN WONDERING THIS FOR A WHILE, BUT... WHAT IS THAT THING?

WHY WOULD A MANJU STEAMED BUN SPEAK?

AND FINALLY ...

THIS IS KURO-PUU!

THAT'S "KUROGANE"!!

CHU'NYAN-CHAN, HUH? MY NAME'S FAI.

AND...

THIS IS SYAORAN-KUN.

WE HAVE SAKURA-CHAN OVER HERE.

...FOR YOU TO WISH THAT THIS AMEN'OSA WERE TO COME, YOU MUST THINK THIS LEADER OF YOURS IS A BAD MAN.

IN OTHER WORDS...

HE TOOK MY OMONI... MY MOTHER, AND...

HE'S THE WORST!

34

THAT WAS NO NATURAL WIND...

...JUST NOW.

YES...

FATHER!
ABOJI!
YOU
DID IT!

BUT WHO DO YOU THINK THOSE PEOPLE ARE?

ABOJI?

NOW THE TOWN OF RYONFI KNOWS THE POWER OF ITS RYANBAN!

YAY!

THEY COULDN'T REALLY BE AMEN'OSA, COULD THEY?

Chapitre.16
Empty Memory

RESERVoir CHRoNiCLE

IS IT ALL RIGHT TO TAKE THE PRINCESS OUT LIKE THIS?

YOU NEVER KNOW IF SHE'S ROWING THE BOAT OR ASLEEP AT THE OAR.

HA HA HA HA!

CHU'NYAN-CHAN OFFERED TO TAKE SAKURA-CHAN AND SYAORAN-KUN ON A RECONNAIS-SANCE MISSION.

MOKONA MIGHT BE ABLE TO SENSE SOMETHING.

AWW, DAMMIT!

WHY DOES THAT STUPID MANJU BUN HAVE TO BE ON THAT BRAT'S SHOULDER ALL THE TIME?!

EVEN THOUGH IT *DOES* SEEM THAT A FEW MEMORIES HAVE RETURNED.

SHE'S ONLY BEEN ABLE TO RETRIEVE TWO FEATHERS.

SHE DOESN'T HAVE ENOUGH MEMORIES YET...

...TO RETURN TO THE OLD SAKURA-CHAN AGAIN.

48

SO...

IN ANY CASE, IT'S OUR JOB TO MAKE REPAIRS WHILE WAITING FOR THEM TO COME HOME.

I WONDER IF THEY'LL BRING PRESENTS?

HM?

WHERE DOES THAT GIVE YOU THE RIGHT TO RELAX AND DRINK TEA?!

GET TO WORK!!

BUT...

...I'M SUPERVISING KURO-PIPPI'S HARD WORK!

49

DO YOU FEEL A POWER WAVE FROM A FEATHER?

MOKONA CAN'T TELL.

The Country of KORYO

"WEIRD POWER"?

THROUGH THIS WHOLE COUNTRY...

...MOKONA FEELS IT FILLED WITH A WEIRD POWER!

HO, CHU'NYAN!

YOU'RE DRAGGING AN OUTSIDER AROUND TOWN, HUH?

I'VE SEEN SOMETHING VERY MUCH THE SAME AT ONE POINT.

THEY'RE CALLED "SAIKORO" WHERE I COME FROM.

IT'S CALLED NEGI.

DON'T YOU KNOW ABOUT IT?

WHAT IS THIS?

OHO! TRAVELERS!

WILL YOU JOIN US?

THEY'RE GUESTS!

THEY CAME FROM A LONG WAY AWAY!

AND IF THEY ADD UP TO HAVE MORE DOTS THAN YOUR OPPONENT, YOU WIN!

THROW TWO CUBES.

IT'S EASY!

AAH! IT TALKED!!

WHAT IS THIS?!

MOKONA!!

THEY JUST LOVE THIS GAME! HONESTLY!

THE OLDER MEN DO, ANYWAY!

THEN... WHO IS THE PERSON WHO THREW THE HIGHEST NUMBER?

KLIK KLAK

NOW...

...TEST YOUR LUCK!

51

DADOOOM

I THREW 11!

I DID!

KLKRLL

SHE'S NEVER DONE THIS BEFORE!

WHAT KIND OF GAME ARE YOU PLAYING?!

BUT...THAT MEANS THE ONLY WAY TO WIN IS TO THROW THE HIGHEST NUMBER ON EACH CUBE, TWO SIXES!

KALAANNG

TIME FOR THE NEXT THROW.

I...I GUESS SOME PEOPLE HAVE THE LUCK.

AH... HA HA HA HA HA HA...

WAHOO! SAKURA WON!!

ROLL THEM, YOUNG LADY...

RUBB RUBB

コロン KLAKKLAK

DADOOOM

WRAAAH!

GIVE ME A BREAK !!

?

コロン KLAKKLAK

コロン KLAKKLAK

KLAKKLAK

WHY NOT?

ALL I REMEMBER ...

...IS MY NAME ...

AND ...

...SOME PEOPLE FROM A DESERT TOWN.

THAT'S ALL.

THERE WAS DESERT ALL AROUND US...

...BUT THERE WAS A LITTLE BIT OF LOVINGLY TENDED LAND.

THAT'S ABOUT ALL.

BEYOND THAT, I CAN'T REMEMBER A THING.

YOUR STORE HASN'T PAID THE RYANBAN'S TAX MONEY, HAS IT?!

DON'T! PLEASE!!

MY FATHER IS OLD AND SICK! AND A SICK HARABOJI NEEDS HIS MEDICINE!

ALL I ASK IS FOR YOU TO WAIT A LITTLE WHILE LONGER!

NO MORE WAITING!!

YOU'RE CHARGING TWENTY TIMES WHAT THE OLD RYANBAN CHARGED!

THERE'S NO WAY WE CAN PAY THAT!

WE CAN'T!

YOU WILL PAY ALL OF THE TAXES YOU OWE IN FULL NOW!!

SHE HAD PRIDE IN HER JOB AS A SHINBAN!

BUT SHE WOULD NEVER HAVE USED THAT POWER FOR BAD PURPOSES!

PEOPLE WOULD ASK HER TO MAKE MEDICINES OR CAST CHARMS.

SHE HAD SOME WONDERFUL POWERS!

BUT THAT CREEP AND HIS FATHER...

THEN THEY CHASED THE OLD RYANBAN-SAMA AWAY AND SET THEMSELVES UP AS RYANBAN IN HIS PLACE!

THEY DIDN'T HAVE ANY SPECIAL POWERS, BUT SUDDENLY THEY BECAME VERY POWERFUL!

THEY WERE JUST WANDERING SHINBAN THAT CAME TO TOWN A YEAR AGO!

Chapitre.17
The Source of Magic

68

70

SYAORAN-KUN!!

YOU GET IT NOW?!

THIS IS THE POWER OF THE *RYANBAN!*

YOU HAVE TO CALL FOR YOUR DADDY WHEN YOU'RE LOSING A FIGHT?!

YOU ARE THE WORST EXCUSE FOR A FAMILY I'VE EVER SEEN!

JUST *SHUT UP!!*

IF YOU DON'T LIKE IT, THEN GO AHEAD AND TRY TO BEAT MY ABOJI, CHU'NYAN!!

BUT YOU *CAN'T!*

WHY?

BECAUSE YOU CAN'T EVEN *TOUCH* HIM!!

HA HA

HAAA

HA

73

YAP AWAY ALL YOU WANT!

WHEN AMEN'OSA COMES, ALL OF THE EVIL THINGS THAT YOU TWO HAVE BEEN DOING WILL BE JUDGED!

YOU CAN'T—

AS PUNISHMENT FOR YOUR RESISTANCE, YOUR TAX IS DOUBLED!

IF YOU DON'T PAY, YOUR STORE WILL BE CONFISCATED, AND YOU AND THE OLD MAN WILL RECEIVE 300 LASHES!

THEY'LL NEVER COME!

H HEH!

WELCOME HOME!

HOW DID EVERYTHING GO?

THE FACT THAT I WAS ABLE TO TALK TO KURO-TAN THE WHOLE TIME MEANS THAT YOU MUST HAVE STAYED PRETTY NEARBY.

HMMP?

THUNK

IS SOMETHING WRONG?

I GUESS SOMETHING IS WRONG.

...IF THE RYANBAN IS THIS BAD, WHY HAVEN'T YOU RISEN UP AGAINST HIM?

BUT...

PWP

I SEE...

YOU WERE DEFEATED BY THE WIND OF THIS RYANBAN GUY AGAIN.

WE DID TRY... A NUMBER OF TIMES.

A GREAT NUMBER OF TIMES!

THE RYANBAN'S CASTLE HAS SOME KIND OF MAGIC AROUND IT.

NOBODY WAS ABLE TO GET CLOSE.

BUT WE WERE NEVER ABLE TO SET ONE FINGER ON THE RYANBAN.

BY MY WAY OF THINKING, THAT IDEA IS A LITTLE LATE IN COMING.

HAVE YOU CONSIDERED HOLDING HIM HOSTAGE OR SOMETHING LIKE THAT?

WHAT ABOUT THAT SON OF HIS?

NOW YOU'RE TALKING!

THAT MAKES SENSE!

THAT ACCOUNTS FOR THE WEIRD POWER THAT MOKONA SENSED, DOESN'T IT?

WITH ALL OF THE WEIRD POWER AROUND, MOKONA CAN'T TELL IF THERE IS A POWER WAVE FROM THE FEATHER OR NOT.

THAT WOULDN'T ADD UP.

IT WAS ONLY A SHORT TIME AGO THAT THE MEMORY FEATHERS WERE SCATTERED THROUGH THE WORLDS.

IT'S POSSIBLE THAT TIME FLOWS DIFFERENTLY IN EACH OF THEM.

WE'RE IN DIFFERENT DIMENSIONS.

SYAORAN-KUN, YOU'RE WOUNDED!

I'M FINE!

BUT...

WAIT!

I'LL GO CHECK...

...ON WHETHER THE RYANBAN HAS A FEATHER OR NOT.

JUST WAIT A MOMENT.

THE MAGIC OF THE RYANBAN IS PRETTY STRONG.

IF YOU SIMPLY WALK THERE, YOU'LL NEVER SUCCEED.

AT THE VERY LEAST, WE'LL NEED ENOUGH POWER TO CREATE AN ENTRANCE TO THAT CASTLE.

AH, NO...

YOU CAN RELAX.

IT'S JUST...

I'M NOT TRYING TO STOP YOU.

MOKONA WILL ASK!!

QUIT PRETENDING YOU HAVE A PLAN WHEN YOU DON'T!!

WHO? THE SPACE-TIME WITCH?

IMPOSSIBLE!

VSSH

CAN'T *YOU* DO SOMETHING ABOUT THAT?

I SEE.

THERE ARE LIMITS TO HOW CONVENIENT THINGS SHOULD BE!!

MOKONA SURE IS CONVENIENT AT TIMES!

WE CAN TALK TO DIFFERENT DIMENSIONS!

SEEP!

SO YOU HAVE TO BREAK THROUGH THE MAGIC— IF THAT'S WHAT IT IS— TO ENTER THE CASTLE?

THAT'S THE PROBLEM.

THE MARKINGS THAT MADE UP YOUR PAYMENT TO ME...

...WERE A DEVICE THAT HELD YOUR MAGICAL POWER IN CHECK.

WHY WOULD YOU NEED TO CONTACT ME?

FAI CAN USE MAGIC, CAN'T HE?

I TURNED OVER THE SOURCE OF MY MAGIC TO YOU.

BE THAT AS IT MAY...

...WITHOUT THOSE MARKINGS WHO COULD EXPECT YOU TO BE ABLE TO WIELD YOUR MAGIC?

YOUR MAGIC NOW IS WHAT IT WAS ORIGINALLY MEANT TO BE.

FINE.

I'LL HAND OVER SOMETHING THAT WILL HELP BREAK THE MAGIC ARTS SURROUNDING THE CASTLE.

BUT I'LL EXPECT PAYMENT IN RETURN.

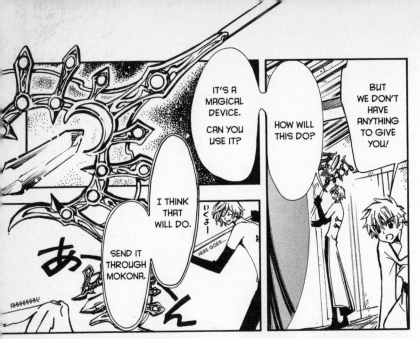

IT'S A MAGICAL DEVICE.

CAN YOU USE IT?

HOW WILL THIS DO?

BUT WE DON'T HAVE ANYTHING TO GIVE YOU!

I THINK THAT WILL DO.

SEND IT THROUGH MOKONA.

HERE GOES...

AHHHHHHHH!

ZUUUUUUUUUU

AAAAAH!

AAAAAAH!

GULP

YES... I'M SURE.

ARE YOU SURE?

BOINK

SLOOM

POP

THIS...

...WILL DEFEAT THE CASTLE'S MAGIC?

86

Chapitre.18
The Castle of Traps

88

THE REASON YOU'RE NOT TAKING CHU'NYAN ALONG...

...IS BECAUSE SHE'S ALREADY SUFFERED TOO MUCH HARDSHIP.

I THINK YOU SHOULD HAVE SAID IT.

I DON'T HAVE ANY STRONG MAGIC...

THE RYANBAN SAW THAT SHE TOOK IN STRANGERS LIKE US, AND IF WE BROUGHT HER TO STORM THE CASTLE...

...AND IF FOR SOME REASON WE AREN'T ABLE TO DEFEAT THE RYANBAN, CHU'NYAN WILL SUFFER THE WORST FOR IT.

......

WHAT HAPPENS IF WE FIND OUT THAT THE RYANBAN DOES HAVE ONE OF SAKURA'S FEATHERS?

SO...

...AND PUT HIM OUT OF OUR MISERY!

HEH

WHATEVER ELSE HAPPENS...

...IT'LL BE BETTER IF WE TAKE THE RYANBAN...

I'LL GET IT BACK!

I WONDER WHAT THAT CHILD HAS HIDDEN?

THOSE FOOLS!

LET THEM COME!

I SENSE A STRONG POWER.

SO, THEY'VE COME.

D—

DON'T WORRY, ABOJI!

NO ONE CAN STAND AGAINST YOUR MAGIC!

94

95

VOING

YOU THROW IT!!

EH?!

...IS THE TIME FOR THE ITEM GIVEN TO US BY THE SPACE-TIME WITCH.

TA-DAAAAAAH

IT LOOKS LIKE A MUDBALL.

HOW'RE WE SUPPOSED TO USE THIS THING?

YOU THROW IT AS HARD AS YOU CAN!

HARD ENOUGH TO HIT THE CASTLE!

DOOOM

WHAT KIND OF PLANS ARE THEY MAKING?

SURE! THAT'LL WORK!

MOKONA, IF I HAVE TO GET IT THAT FAR...

EHEH

AA?

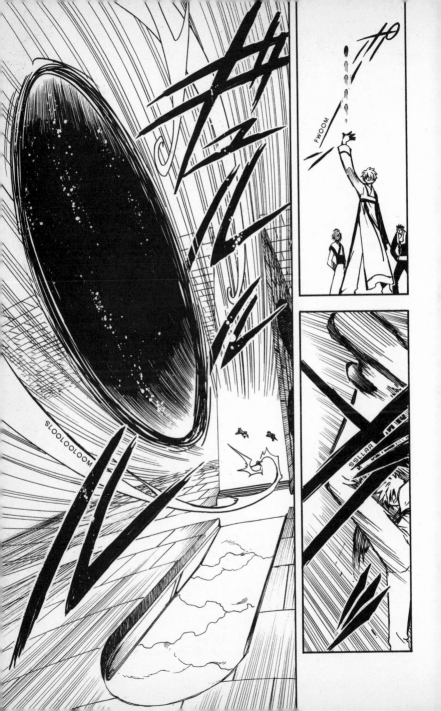

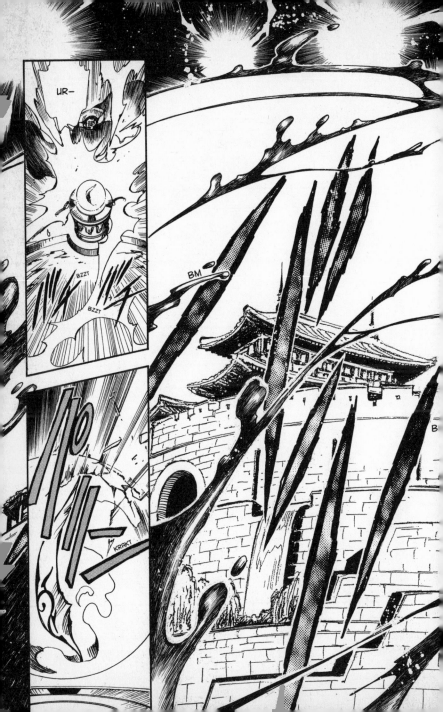

WE'RE BACK WHERE WE STARTED.

I DROPPED THIS ON THE FLOOR AT A SPOT NOT FAR FROM THE ENTRANCE.

I KNOW THIS PLACE LOOKS FAMILIAR, BUT WE NEVER TURNED AROUND!

HM?

IT'S BEEN A ONE-WAY TRIP.

YOU SAID THE WORDS "WHEET-WHOO." YOU DIDN'T WHISTLE.

I'VE BEEN WONDERING ABOUT THAT.

THAT WAS ONE OF THE STONES OF THE GAME THAT FAI AND KUROGANE WERE PLAYING AT CHU'NYAN'S HOUSE!

SORRY, BUT I DON'T KNOW HOW TO WHISTLE.

EH HEH HEH

WHOOO

WHEET-WHOO!

SYAORAN-KUN, YOU'RE GOOD.

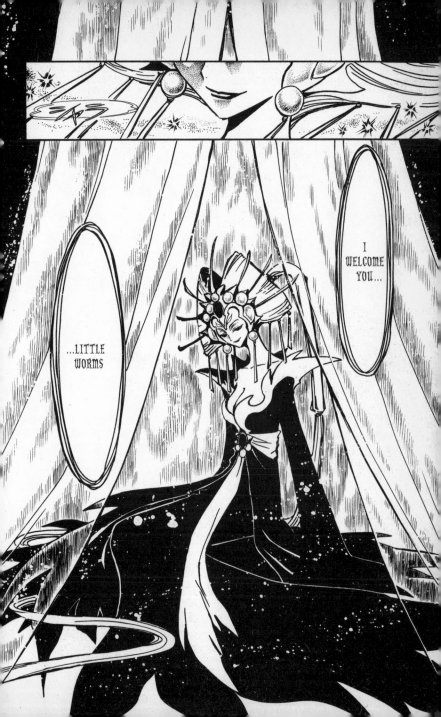

Chapitre.19
The Strongest Kiishim

...BUT IT'S BEEN SO LONG SINCE I HAD A GUEST, I'LL FORGIVE YOUR COARSE TONE.

YOU HUMANS—PATHETIC CREATURES WITH LIVES SPANNING LESS THAN A HUNDRED YEARS—YOU'RE NO BETTER THAN WORMS!

SUCH CREATURES SHOULD WATCH THEIR TONGUES.

WHO THE HELL ARE YOU?!

あ—!? HUH?

WHAT IS SHE SPOUTING?

OR SO I SHOULD SCOLD YOU...

KURO-BUN, YOUR TEMPER IS A LITTLE *TOO* QUICK HERE!

BOTH SHORT-TEMPERED AND SHY! THE COMBO'S PRETTY CUTE!!

THIS IS SUCH A PAIN!

WHATEVER! JUST COUGH UP THE LOCATION OF THAT RYANBAN OF YOURS!

SHE'S CALLING US KIDS!!

TEH HEH

WHAT A NICE COMPLIMENT!

WHAT AMUSING CHILDREN!

I THINK THAT SOMETHING I'M SEARCHING FOR IS IN THIS CASTLE.

WILL YOU PLEASE TELL ME WHERE THE RYANBAN IS?

I LIKE THE LOOK IN YOUR EYES.

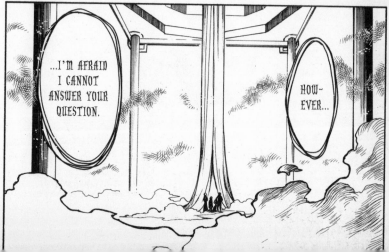

...I'M AFRAID I CANNOT ANSWER YOUR QUESTION.

HOW-EVER...

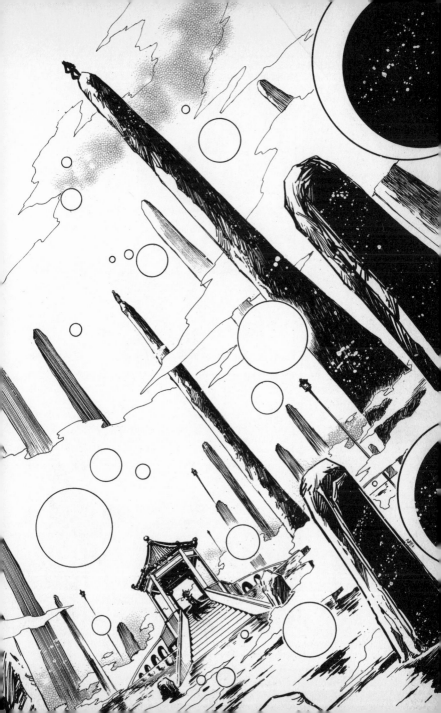

MY LEG!!

THE LAKE AND MY SPHERES ARE MADE OF THE SAME LIQUID.

UMPH!

YOU'RE TELLING ME THAT IF I FALL IN THE LAKE, I'M GONNA MELT?!

OF COURSE...

...NOT EVERYTHING YOUR EYE SEES IS AS IT APPEARS.

WE'RE NOT FINISHED WITH THE BATTLE HERE!

SYAORAN-KUN...

...TAKE MOKONA AND GO ON AHEAD.

NOW...

...WE'LL NEVER GET ANYWHERE PLAYING IN THIS PLAYGROUND.

YOU HAD BETTER MOVE FORWARD WHILE YOUR LEG STILL WORKS.

ALSO...

TRUE.

BUT NUMBERS WON'T HELP IN THIS BATTLE.

SYAORAN-KUN, YOU STILL HAVE UNFINISHED BUSINESS, HAVEN'T YOU?

THANK YOU!

NEVER FEAR!

KURO-PII WILL SAVE THE DAY FOR US!

POFF

ME AGAIN?!

THE MAGIC IS THINNEST ABOVE US.

SYAORAN-KUN, NO DOUBT YOU'LL BE ABLE TO MAKE IT OUT THAT WAY.

I'LL HAVE TO TREAT THE TWO REMAINING CHILDREN WITH MOXIBUSTION.

.....

HUMPH!

I'D SAY OUR SITUATION IS SERIOUS.

SYAORAN!

DOES YOUR FOOT HURT?

IF THAT'S THE CASE...

IT'S FINE.

ZLIP

DOOM

I'M GONNA HAVE TO MAKE SURE YOU CAN NEVER STAND AGAIN!!

Chapitre.20
The Final Battle

RESERVoir CHRoNiCLE

THAT'S RIGHT!

MY ABOJI, THE RYANBAN OF RYONFI TOWN AND THE COUNTRY OF K'ORYO, GAVE ME THIS BODY!

I SENSE THAT WEIRD FEELING FROM HIM REALLY STRONGLY!

THE SECRET ARTS, HUH?

YOU UPSTART LITTLE *BRAT!!*

MOKONA, STAY BACK A WAY.

SYAORAN!

WHOOO

132

133

THAK

SPASSH

I SEE YOUR POINT.

NEXT TIME YOU MOVE ME, DO IT WITH A LITTLE MORE CARE, HM?

IF I DIDN'T, YOU'D BE MELTED BY NOW.

KURO-MU! YOU'RE MEAN!

KAFF

KAFF

SHHHHHHHH

YOU HAVE SOME SKILL, CHILDREN.

BOK

JINNG

IT'S BEEN...

BOK

136

144

AND WE'RE NOT GOING ANYWHERE UNTIL THAT WHITE MANJU BUN FINDS THE PRINCESS'S FEATHER, RIGHT?

SO WE'D BETTER STEP IT UP, AND GET TO OUR NEXT WORLD.

BECAUSE THERE IS A PERSON SLEEPING UNDERWATER WHO, WHEN HE WAKES UP...

...WILL PROBABLY COME AFTER ME.

WHY'S THAT?

PERSONALLY, I DISLIKE STAYING IN ONE PLACE.

146

SYAORAN!

SYAORAN!

GATCH

KYAAA!

WHAT THE HELL IS THIS THING?!

DID YOU CONJURE IT UP WITH MAGIC?!

KYAA!

THE RUMORS ...

...TALK ABOUT THERE BEING PEOPLE IN AMEN'OSA THAT CAN USE MAGIC!

BUT YOU GUYS DON'T REALLY CALL YOURSELVES AMEN'OSA, DO YOU?

153

THE KIISHIM...

...WOUNDED YOU IN THIS FOOT, DIDN'T SHE?

GRNCH

IS IT AGONIZING?

GRIND

GRIND

WELL?

DOES IT HURT?!

IT ISN'T THERE AS GUARD.

YOU AREN'T GONNA BEAT SOMEBODY AS GOOD AS I AM PUTTING UP A WOUNDED LEG AS YOUR GUARD.

YOU LIKE TO USE KICKS WHEN YOU FIGHT.

154

GRR...

KRAKL

THE KIISHIM SHOULD *NEVER* HAVE BEEN DEFEATED!

MY SON...

HE SHOULD BE FINISHING UP HIS JOB BY NOW...

FWAA

IF YOU TRY ANY MORE OF YOUR WEIRD TRICKS...

INSIDE THAT STONE WERE THE MAGICS THAT KEPT ME IN THRALL TO THE RYANBAN.

THAT WAS A THANK YOU.

WHAT KIND OF MAGIC ARE YOU TRYING ON ME NOW?!

162

HAD I THE CHOICE, I WOULD NEVER HAVE DEFENDED THAT BRAINLESS RYANBAN AND HIS SON AGAINST TWO SUCH STEADFAST CHILDREN.

I WAS FINALLY SET FREE.

OH! I SEE.

あーなるほど

AND WHEN KURO-PON SMASHED THE STONE...

AND THE RYANBAN CUR IS ATTEMPTING TO ATTACK WITH...

...YET ANOTHER COWARDLY TACTIC.

HOWEVER, IT SEEMS THAT THE SMALLEST OF YOU CHILDREN HAS ALREADY ARRIVED.

YOU WISHED TO KNOW THE LOCATION OF THE RYANBAN.

HE ABIDES IN THE HIGHEST FLOOR OF THE CASTLE.

ARE YOU HERE ... ... MOKONA ?

YEAH ...

THIS IS WHERE THE WEIRD POWER IS STRONGEST.

BUT MOKONA'S FEELING REALLY DIZZY...

KREEEEEE

IT'S SAKURA'S FEATHER!

YOU WERE ABLE TO DEFEAT MY MAGIC!

THEN YOU *MUST* BE AMEN'OSA.

BOINK

.....
LET THEM DOWN.

EVEN IF THEY DID, THERE'S STILL A GOOD CHANCE THAT I CAN DEFEAT AMEN'OSA, TOO.

WAIT...

SO THEY TOLD THE CENTRAL GOVERNMENT ABOUT ME.

166

SYAORAN!!

JUST SET A FINGER ON ME...

...AND YOU'VE CONDEMNED THEM TO DEATH!!

168

169

Chapitre.21
The Mirror of the
Greatest Love

174

175

177

WHAT WAS THAT?

THAT'S JUST A TRICK, TOO?

DOESN'T CALL ME "SYAORAN."

WH—

WHAT ARE YOU SAYING?

THEY'RE THE TRUE—

HER HIGH-NESS...

YOUR HOSTAGES UP THERE ARE JUST FAKES, AREN'T THEY?

179

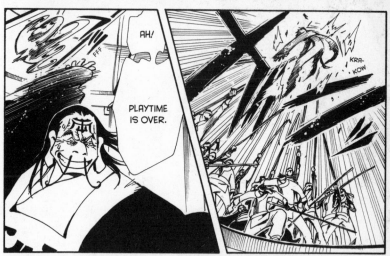

AH!

PLAYTIME IS OVER.

KRA-KOW

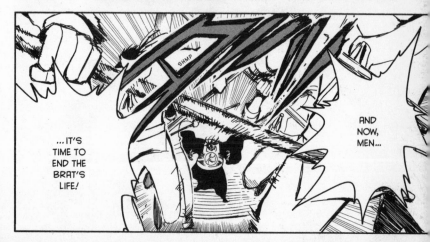

...IT'S TIME TO END THE BRAT'S LIFE!

AND NOW, MEN...

WHAT'S THIS?

IT SEEMS PRETTY CROWDED IN THERE.

GIVE THE FEATHER BACK!

YOU'RE BOTH *LATE!!*

ZOOM

AW, SHADDUP!

IT SEEMS THAT QUITE A BIT HAS GONE ON HERE.

SORRY.

186

...HE SPOUTS SUCH LIES!!

AND STILL...

CHU'NYAN...

DO YOU WANT TO TAKE YOUR REVENGE NOW?

To Be Continued

About the Creators

CLAMP is a group of four women who have become the most popular manga artists in the United Kingdom—Ageha Ohkawa, Mokona, Satsuki Igarashi, and Tsubaki Nekoi. They started out as doujinshi (fan comics) creators, but their skill and craft brought them to the attention of publishers very quickly. Their first work from a major publisher was *RG Veda*, but their first mass success was with *Magic Knight Rayearth*. From there, they went on to write many series, including *Cardcaptor Sakura* and *Chobits*, two of the most popular manga available. Like many Japanese manga artists, they prefer to avoid the spotlight, and little is known about them personally.

CLAMP is currently publishing three series in Japan: *Tsubasa* and *xxxHOLiC* with Kodansha and *Gohou Drug* with Kadokawa.

Translation Notes

Japanese is a tricky language for most Westerners, and translation is often more art than science. For your edification and reading pleasure, here are notes on some of the places where we could have gone in a different direction in our translation of the work, or where a Japanese cultural reference is used.

Tora-Cola

If you will remember from the previous volume, "Tora" means Tiger—the mascot of Osaka's baseball team, the Hanshin Tigers, and the symbol of the entire Hanshin Republic. History buffs might also recognize "Tora" as the Japanese Navy's signal to start the attack on Pearl Harbor: "Tora Tora Tora."

Chu'nyan

What's with the apostrophe? It's just to note that the *n* belongs with "nyan" rather than with "Chu." By the way, "chu" uses the kanji (the Japanese system of writing) for "spring," and "nyan" uses the kanji for "scent."

Ryanban

The "Ry" combination is one of the most difficult combination of sounds for native, monolingual English speakers to wrap their lips around. Many would pronounce "Ryan" as if they were saying the first name of Ryan O'Neal. Not quite. First, remember that the "r"

193

sound in Japanese sounds like a very light "d" sound—similar to the "r" sound that an upper-class British person would use to pronounce the word "very." Add that to a "ya" sound, and you get a single syllable that sounds a little like "dya." Remember, it's not "di-ya" or "ri-ya," but "rya."

Manju

The same type of big, white, wheat-dough bun as Siu Bao found in dim sum restaurants, and sometimes sold steaming hot on a chilly autumn day by street vendors in Yokohama's Chinatown. Mmmm.

Mito Kômon

One of Japan's most popular hour-long TV dramas, "Mito Kômon" began its run in 1970 and continues today. The main character is an elderly aristocrat who travels Japan with his three retainers, finding injustice and doing what he can to correct it. In the last act of every show, just when the bad guys seem to have the upper hand (reportedly at exactly the same minute mark of every program), Mito-sama pulls out the emblem of his nephew, the Shogun! The bad guys

realize that Mito-sama's influence trumps any power they might have, and they capitulate. Like James Bond, the title character has been played by a number of different actors.

Rowing the Boat or Asleep at the Oar

Actually, both of these phrases mean the same thing . . . that Sakura is basically asleep. "Asleep at the oar" is obvious, but "rowing the boat" also means that she's a little brain-numb—probably because of the less-than-towering amount of brain work it takes to row.

Gambling Prizes

Cash payoffs for gambling are illegal in Japan, so you will find that gambling for prizes is a very normal occurrence. Unlike skeeball-style amusement centers in the U.S., the prize counters at pachinko parlors are more like mini convenience stores with food, cigarettes, and household items. In Chu'nyan's country the prizes are a natural product of the barter system, and bringing home groceries from your lucky gambling trip is very common to Japanese readers.

195

Moxibustion

An ancient Chinese remedy, possibly even the precursor to acupuncture, since the Chinese word for acupuncture literally means "acupuncture-moxibustion." A lit and smoldering stick of mugwort is placed on or over an acupuncture point (sometimes to the point of scarring the skin). When combined with acupuncture, the lit mugwort is attached to heat the needle. Like most Chinese medicine, the purpose of moxibustion is to enhance the blood flow and elevate the chi. The Kiishim intends to treat Kurogane and Fai with a full-body acid-based moxibustion, which would almost assuredly be . . . unpleasant.

Mirrors

Mirrors are a traditional mystic element of the earliest parts of Japanese culture. According to

the Kojiki (the book of Japanese myths), the Sun Goddess Amaterasu ordered her son, Ninigi-no-Mikoto, to go to Earth, and with him she sent three sacred objects: a magatama (a beadlike jewel accessory), a sword, and a mirror. Those three objects have been passed down in the Japanese imperial family. Mystical mirrors have also crept into Japan's fox-spirit tales and other traditional stories.

Preview of Volume 4

We're pleased to present you a preview from Volume 4. This volume will be available from Tanoshimi in September 2006, but for now you'll have to make do with Japanese!

よくも私をこんな城に閉じこめてくれたな

ひっ

この領主は私が預かろう

‥‥ゆっくり礼をせねばならん

信用しても大丈夫そうだよ——その秘妖さん

い‥‥いやだ!!

シタバタ

おまえの母親は
良い秘術師だった

この領主の
卑劣な罠によって
亡きものとなったが

私との戦いで
己を磨き

おまえが成長して
そんな己以上の秘術師に
なることを楽しみにしている
と言っていた